Help Me, God, I'm a Parent

Help Me, God, I'm a Parent

HONEST PRAYERS FOR HECTIC DAYS AND ENDLESS NIGHTS

Bunmi Laditan

Bestselling Author of *Dear God*

ZONDERVAN
BOOKS

ZONDERVAN BOOKS

Help Me, God, I'm a Parent
Copyright © 2022 by Bunmi Laditan

Requests for information should be addressed to:
Zondervan, *3900 Sparks Dr. SE, Grand Rapids, Michigan 49546*

Zondervan titles may be purchased in bulk for educational, business, fundraising, or sales promotional use. For information, please email SpecialMarkets@Zondervan.com.

ISBN 978-0-310-36507-5 (hardcover)
ISBN 978-0-310-36511-2 (audio)
ISBN 978-0-310-36508-2 (ebook)

Cover design: Thinkpen Design
Cover illustration: Gizele / Shutterstock
Interior design: Sara Colley

Printed in the United States of America

22 23 24 25 26 27 28 29 30 /LSC/ 12 11 10 9 8 7 6 5 4 3 2 1

To El Roi—
The God Who Sees Me

To M, T, and F—
May you always know His love.

NOTE TO THE READER

I was raised in a religious household and around religious people but can say that while religious ideas may have permeated my mind, they never touched my heart. I know there were some good people of faith around me, but I found myself fixating on the hypocrites, growing angry as I saw them flourish and their harmful actions go unchecked. I felt very little love in religious settings, only the weight of the cultural rules and disdain for those deemed "outsiders" and "sinners." So I became one—an outsider. I wandered. I knew of God but had no relationship with God, and I felt a deep-down hatred for religious people—especially Christians—whom I felt had repeatedly rejected and scorned me.

When I met and married a Jewish man, I was not required to convert to his faith, but I did. My upbringing had instilled in me the value of raising children in one faith tradition, and something about this people who been chased, hunted all over the earth, and yet still believed in God spoke to me. I respected them. I wanted my children to learn their heritage of resilience in the face of extreme persecution. I wanted them to know the importance of *mitzvot* (good deeds) and *tikkun olam* (repairing the world in any small way), and to be able to toast *l'chaim* (to life) even in difficult seasons.

So I studied. I shed the weight of my religious bitterness and embraced the role of a Jewish mother. I was good at it. In fact, I loved it. Fridays were for kneading soft challah dough in my kitchen, my baby strapped to my back, sleeping against the rhythmic folding.

Saturdays were for rest and *shul* (synagogue), where I recited the *Shema* (a daily declaration of faith) and felt the power of the ancient prayer that calls all Israel to set her sights on her Maker: "Hear, O Israel: The LORD our God, the LORD is one."*

I dutifully and joyfully signed up my oldest for Hebrew camp, decorated Hanukkah cookies, dressed with *tzniut* (modesty), fasted on Yom Kippur, and studied Hebrew. I was content, happy in fact, in my new tribe.

When the marriage ended, however, I found myself floating. Suddenly the faith that had bound our family felt like a cruel joke.

I spent the next few years spiraling in and out of mental and emotional crises. I still occasionally baked challah but never felt the same lightness of spirit when I did. I observed whatever holidays the culture around me deemed important, but I never prayed.

Did I mention I was living in a new city, a new country, and barely knew a soul? And yet something kept me afloat. I was always aware of a feeling of being seen and loved but didn't know where it came from. Luck? Karma? Nature? I didn't know. A few years later, after having another child in a relationship that ended, I was once again on my own. Putting my hope in relationships hadn't worked. Putting my faith in any and every religion I could find—from paganism to multiple religions—had worked for a while but ultimately left me feeling lost. So I decided to go to the Source.

I prayed. Wearing jeans and a hoodie, I approached the throne of a God I wasn't even sure existed and asked, "Who are You?"

---

* Deuteronomy 6:4.

And He answered.

Today, my Friday afternoons are filled with rushing to prepare for Shabbat, my three children giggling and playing as they anticipate their favorite day of the week—the one with no chores! My mind swirls with all the things I need to do: sweep the floors, make sure the *cholent* (stew) is going in the slow cooker so we have a warm meal on the one day I don't cook, and have the kids learn the *parsha* (weekly Bible portion). My mind is at peace. Not because I feel enveloped in the safety of a community or religion, but because I know *Him*.

In my house, we call Him *Yeshua*. You may know Him as Jesus. To me, He's not a historical or political figure; He's my brother, friend, and literal savior. I'm aware that, to many, my life may seem anything from strange to blasphemous.

It's only when I leave our cozy home that I sometimes feel as if I walk between two worlds—a mainstream Christian one with whom I share a Messiah, and a mainstream Jewish one with whom I share a painful history, daily life traditions, and relentless faith. It's not always easy, but I count myself blessed to finally know the peace that covers all circumstances.

If you'd have told me ten or twenty years ago that I'd say all this, I would have called you a liar. But all it takes is one encounter with the Carpenter from a tiny, unimportant fishing village, a Messiah who loves like no one else, to be forever changed. It was through Him that I finally and truly began to know God.

And the journey began.

Come along if you'd like.

Love, Bunmi

CONTENTS

A FEW WORDS
BEFORE YOU BEGIN

If you're reading this, it's because you're a parent, a grandparent, an uncle, an aunt, a caregiver in these wild and crazy times. And you need a little (or maybe a lot of) extra help.

Raising and pouring love into a child is an amazing calling. But let's be honest: it's also incredibly difficult.

Caring for children stretches our patience, fries our brains, and zaps us of our energy, but we wake up and do it over and over again because, well, they're ours and we love them.

Before I became a believer in Jesus, I dealt with the stress in every possible way except prayer. I'd binge-watch TV series looking for escape, indulge in glass after glass of wine trying to numb my brain, climb to the pinnacle of my career, thinking money and the approval (envy) of others would give me fulfillment. But I found none of what I sought.

Who would have thought that a relationship with God would be the key? And there is no relationship without communication.

Prayer became my lifeline.

I thought prayer was no different from positive affirmations, thoughts we throw into the air and hope stick somewhere.

Now I know different.

And behold, I am with you always, to the end of the age.

Matthew 28:20

When I pray, I know God is by my side. He is there, not passively listening, but hearing me, responding, and sending comfort, help, peace, solutions, and love.

Do not be anxious about anything, but in everything by prayer and supplication with thanksgiving let your requests be made known to God.

Philippians 4:6

As a child to a parent, I pray to a loving, protective, attentive God who is always near. Sometimes I'm asking for help, other times I'm marveling at the hilarity and beauty of parenting, and other times I'm just thanking Him for the many ways He's shown me signs of His provision and love.

Pray without ceasing.

1 Thessalonians 5:17

I have a new habit. When I wake up, before the chaos begins, I resist grabbing my phone and instead close my eyes and pray. I thank God for waking us up and keeping us safe in the night, and ask for help, protection, and direction for this day.

Before bed, we pray as a family, again thanking God for being with us during the day—and whatever else we'd like to tell Him.

But the times I pray the most . . . well, all day—as I'm driving, making my way through traffic, standing at the kitchen sink with rubber-gloved hands in soapy water, or making dinner. Sometimes my prayers are three-word pleas—"Help me, God"—and other times, I just talk to Him.

We don't have to raise our children alone. In fact, we never will. God has reminded me so many times, especially when I'm afraid or worried, that before they were mine, these children were His. He loves them with a love we can't even imagine.

I hope that in reading these very real prayers that I prayed as a parent, you are inspired to approach the throne of God with your own prayers for little or big ones.

Praying for our children is a powerful act of love. Prayer changes situations. He's listening. He loves you and the little hearts in your care.

Love, Bunmi

WONDER

DEAR PARENT,

Do you ever bask in the wonder of this calling? Whether it's gazing at the deliciously long eyelashes of a sleeping child or feeling your heart nearly burst at the sound of your child's unabashed, full laughter . . . how did we get here? With them? Doing this? Yes, it's so hard, but it's also so beautiful. These prayers express marvel at these awe-inducing moments and reflect on God as a heavenly Father. I hope today you experience one, two, or five moments you want to hold on to forever.

LOVE, BUNMI

1

Dear God,

If there's one thing parenting has taught me,
it's the ferocity of Your love,
because if You love me more than I love them,
Your love must be a roaring flame,
white-hot lightning,
a hundred-foot wave.
Your love is the greatest of all the world's wonders.
How splendid it is to be called
a child of God!

Yours always,
Me

DEAR GOD,

It was raining outside today and my little one wanted to hold our single umbrella.

I gently took it from his small hand and said, "Let me hold it for you. I'm higher up. Just stay underneath," and I knew You had said the same thing to me time and time again. You're saying it now.

I love when You do that.

Thanks for holding the umbrella.

Love,
ME

DEAR GOD,

I see what You're doing. You speak to me when I speak to them.

When I say, "If you had just listened to me . . ." "Trust me, I'm trying to help you."

I hear You.

Is this why You gave them to me? Did You want me to know how hard and beautiful and frustrating and joyful it is to love children?

I do.

My weary heart explodes with love at their sleeping faces. My eyes flash with anger when they willingly disobey. My chest heaves with mercy when I see them, a lamb caught in a briar bush, when they need my help to escape self-inflicted trouble . . . again . . . and again.

I'm not You, but we have something in common, it seems. Our love for these wild ones.

Love,
ME

DEAR GOD,

When I watch them playing happily together, their laughter joining together in the sweetest harmony, it's a little bit of heaven.

In those moments, I know how much You wish we could set aside our differences and come together as Your children. If we could all feast together under Your banner, how it would make You smile.

Help us, Father, to put down our weapons and pick up Your bread. Help us lower our shouts and lift up our voices in praise. Help us.

We love to fight. Help us to love You more.

Love,
ME

Dear God,

You are the Most High, Master of the universe, Creator of all things.

And yet You wanted to be a Father. You wanted someone to call You God—knowing the grief it would cause You, the nights You'd be fighting for them while they fight against You, knowing how much this love can hurt.

Is it because when we smile at You, it warms Your whole heart?

Is it because of how amazing it is to see a child win a battle that beat them yesterday?

Is it because this love—it makes the hardest days worth pushing through?

I won't pretend to understand what it's like to be You, but I do understand one thing.

This love is worth it.

Love,
Me

Dear God,

As I watch the tired parents sitting on park benches at
    4:45 p.m.,
drawing on the final reserves of their energy to smile at the
    child yelling,
"Look what I can do!"
I'm filled with love.

They're so tired, God.
So exhausted.
Surely days weren't meant to be this long.
Or maybe we weren't meant to do this much.

But there's something beautiful
about the weary dedication
of parents,
the worn-out devotion,
a love held together
with frayed patches
of mismatched fabrics.

It's not fancy,
polished,
or perfect,

only determined
to make it to the daily finish line
of bedtime.

It's a daily offering of love
for a child.

Afternoon after endless afternoon
they give.

Please bless them with grace enough.

Love,
Me

Dear God,

Do You watch Your adult children—
us children who have children?
Do You watch us sleep the way we watch our own?

Do You ever hope we'll doze for five more minutes,
knowing when our eyes open,
trouble begins?

Does Your heart burst with joy
when we learn something new?

Do You hold our hands as we take tentative, fresh steps,
wobbling and waddling?

Do You sigh into Your hands
when we stubbornly
refuse,
shout "No!"
tearfully pout,
sleepily whine,
run in tired circles?

Do You ever put us to bed,
cause our eyes to grow heavy,
knowing that what we need
is just rest?

What's it like being a Father to
so many?

. . . If no one has given You one today—

hugs.

Thank You.

We love You.

Sorry for the mess.

ME

DEAR GOD,

I'm amazed at what love can accomplish.

Love got me out of bed at 3:44 a.m. when I heard a tiny knock on my bedroom door. A small child who needed the warmth of my arms.

It's love, not coffee, that made me move the wet clothes into the dryer and cut up yet another apple, arranging it on a small plate.

Love made You come into this world, live, die, and rise again for children who, more often than not, don't get it right.

Love is holding this whole thing together.

You're quite the romantic, aren't You?

Love,
ME

Dear God,

You've watched my family line since the first generation.
You've seen the tree grow, sprout, split, and bear all kinds
    of interesting fruit.
And now the twinkles in my eye are basking in the sun,
stretching their branches
and shooting forth rich green leaves daily.

What must this all look like to You?

May each bough be better than the last.

Love,
ME

Dear God,

It feels as if I'm always trying
to push the scared one out of the nest
and keep the one who doesn't look
before they leap
from hurtling toward the hard soil.
I don't know how You do this with
billions upon billions
of baby birds.

Love,
Me

Dear God,

I look up at the sky
at the clouds,
this moving oil painting we get to
behold every day.
No one ever says,
"Oh great, another sunset."

It's a sight,
a wonder,
a work of art
every single day.

There's no museum with
anything as fine.

And it's free
for all
who will simply look up.

Much like You.
There.
Being God.

Loving and beautiful,
waiting for us to simply
look up.*

ME

---

* See Psalm 121:1.

ENDLESS NIGHTS

Dear parent,

We've all been there.

Whether you're lying down next to a sick child listening to labored breathing, waiting for a sixteen-year-old to walk in well past curfew, or simply dreading taking a fearful child to the dentist tomorrow, these prayers are for calm and peace, and to remind us whose hands it's safe to leave our fears in.

Some nights are hard because we have children who need us past business hours. If this is you, if you're awake by the light of the moon, take heart. You're not alone. My prayer for you is rest. Today. Tomorrow. Soon.

We'll get through this, and we're never alone.

Love, Bunmi

DEAR GOD,

Some days I feel like the parent. And other times, bedtime, for example, when we're curled up reading stories and my tank is running on fumes alone, I'm reminded that I'm a child too. Yours. In the scheme of things, I'm not much older than they are. In Your eyes, am I simply their big sibling, doing my best with the souls entrusted to me for a time?

Aren't all parents really "babies raising babies" under the light of the Father's love?

I may have a bit more experience, but You and I both know I'm winging it. Allow me to hear the wisdom of Your Spirit and do right by these little ones.

Love,
ME

DEAR GOD,

I still wake up to make sure everyone's breathing. I have no idea how You manage with billions of us. It's a good thing You don't sleep because the amount of coffee You'd need would be insane.

Love,
ME

Dear God,

For you formed my inward parts;
>you knitted me together in my mother's womb.
I praise you, for I am fearfully and wonderfully made.

Psalm 139:13–14

And when a child isn't like the others? When a doctor gives a diagnosis with a label, what then? Are they still fearfully and wonderfully made?

I already know the answer to this. Because while in this life, bodies are born without parts that make life possible, children get sick, their spirits land but for a small while. Others struggle with friends and in school because their thoughts are formed differently than their peers'. And others need medication to function in the way that would serve them best.

They are still all perfect.

Their souls are still perfect.

Even if they cannot do so here, there exists a place where they will one day live, run, and play in perfect wholeness and with perfect peace.

All of Your children are fearfully and wonderfully made. Every last one of them.

Love,
Me

DEAR GOD,

What do You say to the mother who said goodbye to her heart? Or the father whose hands hold only the memories of their dreams? Is it the same thing You said to the storm? "Be still."*

Waters rage here, God. They pour down in oceans from the eyes of the mourning. For as long as their hearts beat, parents never stop saying goodbye.

I know You can see them. I can feel Your love for those who weep, whose chests burn with the deepest of losses.

My prayer is this: Please still their storms. Wrap their memories in tender love and put Your arms around them. Wrap peace like a blanket around their shoulders. Please send them butterflies.

Whisper to them of heaven.

Love,
ME

---

* Mark 4:39.

DEAR GOD,

Give me victory in my own battles so they don't become theirs. Show me where I'm wrong, what I'm missing, and where I need to retrace my steps and cut down generational trees that shouldn't have been left standing. Prune me thoroughly so that all I give to them are treasures.

Let me be a higher place for them to start their journey.

Love,
ME

DEAR GOD,

Show me what I need to renounce,
what learned ties I need to cut,
and adopted devils I need to send
to waterless places.

Show me anything not of You
in or around me,
things I've honored, accepted, or
dressed up and given
rooms in my heart.

Show me that which needs
expelling
or healing
so that I can live
and raise these children from a place
of freedom,
victory, and wholeness.

I've seen how
the strange fruit of one generation
becomes the main dish of the next.

That will not be the portion of my children.
In Your name.

ME

DEAR GOD,

I look back and all I can see are the mistakes. So many of them. Too many for them to be okay, right? God, what have I done to Your masterpiece?

My prayer today is that You forgive me for all the ways I got it wrong and count it not against them. Heal them of any wound I've inflicted, any word I shouldn't have said, any decision that was the wrong one, any bad seed I planted. Pull it up.

Rain down grace.

Forgive my mistakes in and around their lives.

Show me how to do better. Help me to love like You, trust like You, and parent like You. Be with me in the trenches today and every day.

Love,
ME

DEAR GOD,

I know I'll never be
one of those parents who can even
pretend to have it all together

My mess is unhidden
chaos unwrapped
mistakes, noisy

So help me
to at least
be good at spotting
and loving the ones
who need it

If I can't inspire
help me to
comfort

ME

Dear God,

Life is so hectic
I'm struggling to keep my own head above water
so I know You must be here
steering the ship,

Had Your hands not been covering the wheel
we would have wrecked miles ago

Had Your will not held these planks together
we'd be resting on the ocean floor

You are here. I cannot see Your face and sometimes I feel almost swallowed by the just-slightly-kept-at-bay chaos, but based on the fact that I'm still standing and they're still smiling and laughing, hoping, You're still here.

Thank You for holding it all together. Please don't ever let us go.

Love,
Me

DEAR GOD,

On the days I feel too broken by life to parent, You parent us both. As I hide my weary tears, hoping they don't see and worry, Your grace spreads out like a blanket, keeping us both warm.

Cover us with Your feathers. Let us find refuge under Your wings.*

On days like this I know that while I have a baby bird, I am Your baby bird too.

Gather us close to Your side and let us close our eyes in relief against Your steady heartbeat.

Love,
ME

Dear God,

I'm thankful for time keeping its steady march into the future. If not for time, I would get stuck too long in the hard places and make a permanent heaven out of the sweet ones.

It's hard seeing their faces grow from soft to angular, baby talk to defiant speeches, but time keeps us moving into Your calling for our lives.

Time has stolen onesies and footie pajamas from me, but it's given me the privilege of seeing wisdom bloom behind young eyes.

Because You know this world needs loving, strong warriors for today. For tomorrow.

Help me to make my peace with time as it brings me ever closer to Your rest.

Love,
Me

Dear God,

I've tried running on:
sheer will,
caffeine,
motivational speeches,
positive affirmations,
religious mantras,
guilt,
human logic,
manic energy,
and image.

All of them failed,
ran out,
backfired,
left me worse off than before.

And then I tasted Your
peace,
sampled Your
loving-kindness,
gave myself to Your
healing forgiveness.

I have been emptied of all
false fuels.

Your Spirit sustains me
on this long but short,
often painful journey.
Your Spirit sustains me.

Stay.

Love,
ME

DEAR GOD,

Please hold their eyes closed tonight.
Suspend them in deep, restful slumber until past dawn.
Send angels to form a boundary around their beds.
Write a pact between their heads and their pillows.
Seal a night of peace for my home—
just one night of promised peace.

ME

DEAR GOD,

A few months ago, my glasses broke.
I was able to piece them together,
but the lens was scuffed.

Whatever I looked at
was obstructed,
just a little bit,
by four tiny scratches.

A bowl of apples
with scratches,
playing children
with scratches,
a gorgeous peachy sunset
with scratches.

God, I know there are scratches
on my heart
from where I fell down.
They make everything
a little less beautiful,
find shadows where none exist,

and cause me to treat
gifts with suspicion.

Today
God,
please give me Your vision.
Let me see some of the beauty
of this life—
unobstructed,
untainted.
Heal my vision.

Love,
ME

DEAR GOD,

By now You're used to me creating
personal hells of my own imaginings,
torment between my ears.

These meals of worst-case scenarios
poison my soul
and eviscerate my peace—
dreadful dessert

Help me to stop.
Sufficient for the day
are its own problems.*

I'm full.

Love,
ME

---

* See Matthew 6:34.

DEAR GOD,

You taught me, in the tender way You do, that it is impossible to parent from a place of wholeness until we have forgiven our own parents.

Whether their crime was simply being human,
or something more egregious,
forgiveness must take place
because it's in the space of unforgiveness
that we unconsciously become that which marked us.

You taught me that forgiveness doesn't mean it didn't
        happen;
it doesn't mean it was okay;
it means I'm letting it go.

I'm letting it go
over and over,
no matter how many times it takes,
until peace replaces unwanted songs on repeat.

I'm letting it go
and allowing Your living waters

to wash over old wounds,
cleanse, and heal.

I'm letting it go
so that Your soft and warm breath of life
can blow power into limp sails,
drawing me nearer to the horizon,
to the dawn where Your Spirit resides
and where I rest.

I'm letting it go
so that the love I have for my children is not tainted
by bitterness
but flows freely from You
through me
to them
without barriers.

I'm letting it go because
I want to be free.

Love,
Me

Dear God,

Please forgive my attitude,
my demands.
I know You're not a genie in a bottle
or a vending machine.
I know what it is to be asked
for a snack every forty-five minutes.
Help me be still and know that
You are God.
Snack or no snacks,
You are God of this situation
and the next.

Me

Dear God,

I have reached the age my parents were
and realize that they were children
raising children.

I forgive them for the mistakes of youth,
the errors fear produces,
the anger depression creates.

I forgive them because I, too, am scrambling,
wondering, worrying, staring into the dark long after
    bedtime,
hoping,
resolving to do better tomorrow.

But most of all, I forgive them because
You forgave me.
They are not gods.
Only You are.

Love,
Me

Dear God,

Hold my parents.
Soothe them
if anywhere in their minds is a tormenting demon
whispering that my mistakes are their fault
or that they could have done better.

Let them know I get it now.
Gift them with peace
and add my name to the card.

I know now that the only perfect parent
in existence
is You,
and I am simply grateful
they tried.

As a parent now, I know nothing just happens—
meals shopped for, paid for, planned,
clothes purchased, mended, and washed.

Thank You, God, for parents who did their best.
Hug them. Let them know it's okay. Let them know it
was a hard job well done.

Love,
Me

DEAR GOD,

I run around
like a chicken with no head,
doing the things
I can barely remember signing up for.
When the day is done
and the house deliciously quiet,

Remind me to choose You
over things that promise to numb
my mind, and whisk me away
to all manner of imaginings.

Remind me that You've been
waiting all day for a quiet
moment with me.

Remind me that in You
is an open invitation
to the place of grace and true rest.

If I'll only look up
and say
yes.

Love,
ME

DEAR GOD,

How can I grow tired of repeating
the same phrases and
commands
over and over—
"Wash your hands."
"We don't hit."
"Can you say please?"—

when I know You've
repeated Yourself just as often to me:
"You're cared for."
"I love you."
"I've got this."
"It will work out."*
"I'll lead you through this"?

How many times do You have to
tell me the same things
before I simply know it to be true?

What in my heart causes Your promises
to evaporate like morning dew
every time a new monster arises?

_____

* See Romans 8:28.

I will stay close to Your streams of
faithfulness and goodness,
and I will drink.

ME

DEAR GOD,

Sometimes it's not the nights. It's the long afternoons after the long nights. When my eyes struggle to stay open and my mind processes at the speed of molasses. I want nothing more than to strip off this uniform and climb back into bed, but it's barely after noon.

I already know You'll see me through it because I've been here before.

But this job. It's like no other.

Coffee? You and me? Tell me how the stars look today.

Love,
ME

DEAR GOD,

How do You do it—watch us walk into the lion's den when You know we'll get bitten? If I could swathe them in bubble wrap and raise them on a deserted tropical island with Wi-Fi and pizza delivery, I would.

How do You do it—watch free will allow a child You love more than the sun to take a giant step toward a cliff?

Do You ever yell? Scream into Your pillow? Or is that why You created angels? For those moments we choose wrong. Heavenly hall monitors. Please keep them coming.

Love,
ME

PROTECTION

DEAR PARENT,

I pray prayers of protection over my children every day, night, and in between. They come out as pleading, as quiet chords, sometimes fearful but always rooted in the promise that faith can move mountains and thereby shadows unknown. It's become my routine to bathe my children in prayers, to beseech God on their behalf, to ask for grace unseen for whatever they may face every day.

I can't be everywhere, but I know Who can be. I don't believe there is a prayer more powerful than from a parent for their child because it echoes the love we have for them. My prayer for you is that you know the power your prayers have and that you will approach the throne on behalf of the little (or big) ones you love.

LOVE, BUNMI

DEAR GOD,

I fail them in small ways every day and in big ways at least
   once a season.

Thoughtless words leave small but lasting fissures,
shortcomings leaving pockets of hunger in their hearts.

Father, if I can do one thing right, it is to point them
   to You.
Your love can cover where mine stops short.
It can heal what mine breaks.
You can bestow on them an inheritance of grace—not
   from my coffers but from heaven.

If I fail in all things but put Your name in their mouth, let
   it be enough.
If I fail in all things but show them how Your love has
   changed me, let it be enough.
If I fail in all things but teach them to call on You when
   there's no one else left, let it be enough.

Let it be enough for them to place their soft hands
   in Your strong ones.

Love,
ME

Dear God,

What a wicked world I have brought my children into. What have I done? I ask, no, I beg of You, to watch and protect them every day of their lives. Send them angels to keep them on the right path. Guard their hearts, souls, bodies, and minds from the evil that lurks like a fog everywhere we turn.

If I had known what this world contained, would I have brought them here? I don't know. But they're not mine; they're Yours, just like I'm Yours. Your love for them endures long after mine goes to bed for the night. Your love neither slumbers nor sleeps.* It eclipses mine. Makes it look like a hobby.

But I do love them.

Please watch over them where and when I can't.

Love,
Me

---

* See Psalm 121:4.

DEAR GOD,

On days they're not with me, I know they're still with You. Please hold them when I can't. Speak to them when my voice is far away. Fill them with Your love when mine is out of reach. And as always, protect them, Lord.

Love,
ME

DEAR GOD,

I pray tonight that You'd reach into the hearts and minds of my children and pull out every harmful seed planted. Pull it out by the roots. Let their soil be so rich with Your love and truth that bad things can't grow there. Till their earth and let it be rich. Please let the lessons You've given me to pass down take root and grow, bearing fruit that they not only can enjoy but can feed others with.

Make in them good gardens.

Love,
ME

DEAR GOD,

When they're crawling, we wish they would walk; when they walk, we can't wait for them to run—and then one day, without even asking, they grow wings.

And we realize how high the sky really is.

I'm scared, God. Because I know what's up there and how hard one can fall.

I ask You, as they fly, cover them with Your wings. Soar with them. Follow them into every cave and through narrow branches. Teach them to hear Your voice over the wind.

Go to the places I can't, God. Just like You did for me. Fly with them.

ME

DEAR GOD,

I never imagined I'd be raising children in a time so frightening. Every day, the ground shifts under our very feet.

The headlines shout threats.

Tomorrow feels like a promise of more trouble on the horizon.

These children have seen too much, experienced too much.

What will become of them?

Nothing surprises You, and as I pray, I feel You whispering to me that You designed them to be strong. You fortified their hearts and bones for such a time as this.*

Did we unknowingly give birth to warriors?

Even so, God, they are so small. So precious.

I've seen the changes these times have written on their faces and souls.

I ask You for protected moments of innocence for them. Yes, they must be strong, but let them have shreds of yesteryears hidden somewhere in their hearts that they can take out like a jewelry box ballerina and delight in.

They have always been Yours before they are ours.

Hold them close.

Love,
ME

---

* See Esther 4:14.

DEAR GOD,

These children consume so much these days, and I'm not talking about food. Through their eyes and ears, information, images, ideas . . . many lies barrel toward their hearts and minds, and I'm afraid. I'm afraid that bad seeds, poisonous plants, will take root. Vines that will squeeze out everything I've poured into them. Vines that will convince them that evil is good. Vines that will tell them they're one purchase away from the perfect peace only You give.

Lord, I can't keep away every message. As they grow, the hearts You've helped me protect must make their way through this jungle of noise. Where my feet can't go, may my prayers fly.

I pray that the belt of truth* stays firmly in place and that You will grace them with razor-sharp discernment. I pray that the truth is their shield and buckler.** I pray that as they navigate the information highway, the Spirit who lives in them will guide them and keep them from harm.

And when they find themselves in places they shouldn't be, seeing things that harm their souls, I pray that You will rescue them and heal them with Your living waters.

These times are not for the faint of heart, and I know You have made these children strong, so I am not afraid. But be with them.

Thank You.

AMEN

---

* See Ephesians 6:14.
**See Psalm 91:4.

Dear God,

Protect me from the voice that whispers, "It's not enough."
Let me not be broken down by feelings of futility.
I know that You can bless even the most meager offerings.
You turn water into wine and snacks into feasts.*
Your power is made perfect in my weakness.**
I am certainly not enough, but Your grace is sufficient and
    You are here with me in the chaos when my patience is
    running thin and my hope is but a sliver.
You lift my arms when I can't.
You provide love when I can't manufacture it.
You are enough, and I am in You.
Help me remind those whispers who's boss. You are.
Stay.

Love,
Me

---

* See John 2:9.
**2 Corinthians 12:9.

DEAR GOD,

I heard someone say once that children pick their parents. That can't be true because there are children in terrible situations.

How do You decide who goes where?

Is it random?

Is there a lottery?

One day, when we're alone, You'll have to explain this to me. It's one of my many questions (including why mosquitos exist).

Tonight, please hold close the parents parenting from a place of wishing they had been loved better.

Please hold close the children who need to be held.

Rescue them.

Bless them and keep them, tonight and always.

Please, one day soon, bring them a joy they didn't know they were worthy of.

Love,
ME

DEAR GOD,

Some nights I'm afraid to fall asleep. Afraid to pull my consciousness away from the children, lest some terror that stalks by night slithers in under my unwatchful gaze. I'm past checking for breathing at 2:00 a.m.—pure exhaustion took care of that—but minutes before my head hits my pillow, when I do my final checks for the rising of chests, fear grips me.

I remind myself that it's not me who has kept them; it's Your will, Your angels, Your plan that has been my saving grace for reasons I won't understand until heaven, but sometimes . . . sometimes I fancy myself the dam that's holding back the floodwaters of the unknown.

And then, after checking the back and front doors again, then the stove and unplugging the toaster, I remember that it's You.

It's You.

It has to be You.

So I pray,

"Watch over us all until my eyes open at dawn,"

And You did. For another night.

Thank You.

Love,
ME

DEAR GOD,

Malevolent arrows will fly,
and we all take the stage
of humiliation at least once in this life.
But I pray that these moments they face
do not seep into their souls
and wound their innermost being.

Please wrap Your hands around their hearts.
Guard the deepest parts of them

so that no matter
whatever comes,
they can feel the difference between
what happened
and who they are.

Love,
ME

DEAR GOD,

Today I wonder if I might lose. It feels as if every power in the air wants them. These influences play a seductive song. It's a better beat than anything I can come up with. It's fast and smooth, pleasing to the ears. Mine is old Truth on a rusty record player.

I may lose, Lord. Help me. Help them.

My strength is not enough. My lyrics and melodies are not enough.

Lord God, they are my only treasure in this earth, but I yield them to You. Because my song is not enough.

I yield them to You.

You made them. These lines are Yours.

Speak to them, Father. Whisper truth into their hearts. Move Your Spirit within them, and let it light their eyes.

Lord, work in their hearts and minds. Give them Your wisdom and let them see with Your vision. Let truth ring supreme and drown out all the noise this world calls music.

Lord, Your will be done. This, my heart, the ones I'm tempted to love more than You.

I yield.

ME

FUTURE

Every night after my children are settled into bed, I ask God to go ahead of us for tomorrow. I know it doesn't mean there won't be challenges, but in this asking, I am reminded that there's nothing we face that He won't be in. I ask God to keep my children on the right path and help them make the decisions that will honor their position as sons and daughters of the Most High.

The world is a scary place, but as I pray over their futures, both near and far, I feel as if I am asking His cloud of grace to abide with them wherever they go.

Remember, even when you're not with them, they're never alone.

Love, Bunmi

Dear God,

Following You isn't risk-free. There are the shocked looks. The ones that imply or state outright that we've been brainwashed, are dumb, or an idiot, or worse. We're lumped in with people who have done horrible things. All I'm guilty of is loving You.

Will my children be able to stand up and state the truth and risk being on the outside for You?

Some days it's hard for me, but You're my strength.

I pray that they find their people to give them comfort, and that they'll rest in Your strength alone.

It can be a very lonely walk home.

Stay close to them.

Love,
Me

DEAR GOD,

Ten times a day, I remind myself that they were Yours first. Before I considered them, You knew them. Before I picked a name out of a hat, You had written one on their hearts. Before I knew them, You loved them.

We are both Your children. I'm just a bit older.

Hold us both. It's scary here sometimes.

Love,
ME

DEAR GOD,

Out of all the things I hope to leave them—maybe a bit of money, wise words, memories of warm hugs and afternoons at the park—the most valuable by far is You.

On days when the whole world disappoints and lemons
        won't turn into lemonade,
on nights that seem to last forever and the pain pulses cold
        and unrelenting,
when they don't know who to trust and which way is up,

they'll have You.

You are the resting place, the cleft in the rock.
Under Your feathers there is safety and the peace that
        surpasses understanding.[*]

Be there for them, my God.
Don't let them go.

Love,
ME

---

[*] See Philippians 4:7.

DEAR GOD,

Everyone talks about the first word and first step, but no one talks about the first time we have to let go.

No one talks about the gut-wrenching feeling that they might go in the wrong direction and they're too old to grab by the overalls and lift into our arms away from the fire.

I don't have as much control as I used to, and it scares me.

But You hold the hearts of kings in Your hand, *so surely You can hold my child. I stay up at night and worry until I feel You reminding me who directs the wind, and I begin to pray.*

Help them.

Protect them.

Shield them . . . I know You won't take every blow, but let no arrow so pierce their hearts that it scars them forever.

Send angels, all of the angels, to knock the drug, drink, or tool of destruction from their hands.

Whisper words of love when all they can hear are echoes in the dark.

Be God for them because I've realized that despite seeming to be all-powerful during the toddler years, I am not.

I'm not You.

---

* See Proverbs 21:1.

You have counted every hair on their heads.** Their fingerprints are Your design.

Be with them today and every day; long after my breath is a memory, be with them.

Love,
ME

Dear God,

If there is a generational curse, an ancestral open door that needs to be closed so that my children can walk in freedom, let it be closed in the name of Jesus, Your Child and my King. Close it so that they can walk with lighter steps than I do. Close it so they can know gardens I only dreamed of. Close it so they can be the light I've always known they were meant to be.

Let them walk through this life with no strings attached and no tainted inheritances.

Thank You for the power to speak life into them.

Love,
Me

DEAR GOD,

So much of parenting is talking. Instructing, speaking soothing words, chiding, being encouraging with my words.

But help me know when to be silent so You can speak into my child's soul.

Help me to know when to be still so You can take over.

Hold me and keep me quiet but near when You need space to heal, inspire, and grow them.

They will never know You if I make myself their god.

Whisper to me when it's time to step aside and let You reign in their hearts.

Love,
ME

Dear God,

In a time when people are more polarized
than I've ever seen,
hating their neighbors,
vilifying their family members,
help me model love.
Help my child to resist fear of humans
whose hearts pump the same blood,
beat to the same rhythm,

and whose souls also yearn for peace.

Help us to remember that,
no matter the philosophies and
conclusions,
we all bear Your holy fingerprints.

Love,
Me

DEAR GOD,

We carry small,
high-powered,
shiny computers
in our pockets

but have forgotten how
to look at another human
with any kind of reverence.

Forgive us.
Forgive me.

Create in these children
clean hearts
and renew right spirits
within them.*

Let them be better than we are.

ME

---

* See Psalm 51:10.

Dear God,

In a world that values appearances
above substance,

likes above love,

going with the flow
instead of being set apart,

help me to raise
young men and women
unafraid to follow You,
not the crowd.

Help them to be
rivers of deep waters,
lovers of justice and mercy,
and champions of the vulnerable,
even when it's not recorded.

Plant them in places that need
truth and love.

And help them grow,
for it's You who makes the increase.*

Grow them
gently, God.

Love,
ME

DEAR GOD,

Today I pray that as I raise
Your creation,
my will would yield to
Your plans for this child
who was created for a purpose.

Whisper to me what needs to be said
or done, or not done.

Help me do this masterpiece,
this work of Your hands,
justice.

Love,
ME

HELP

Dear parent,

These SOS prayers—the heavenly 911 calls of intervention, the running to the throne because the experts, doctors, teachers, friends, and books fell short—have changed my life. I have witnessed firsthand how prayer from the depth of our soul changes situations.

Pray until something shifts. Don't stop. This is His child. You are heard.

Love, Bunmi

DEAR GOD,

On the day I saw the angel, I felt how perfect Your love was.
Before that day, I thought a mother's love was the highest of loves,
the purest of loves.
But in the light of Your love, I felt the fear in mine.
Your love is perfect and complete.
My love is impatient and has an agenda.
Your love heals.
My love can damage.
Your love endures.
My love knows limits.
Your love watches through the night.
My love grows thin by the moon and falls into an exhausted sleep.
I'm telling You what You already know so that I can remember
this truth: my love alone is not enough.
To give these children what they truly need, I must raise my babies
in Your light.
Please help.

Love,
ME

DEAR GOD,

In a world where up is down, left is right, and wrong is right, how do I raise children who turn to You for answers? How can I compete with seductive voices and infinite distractions?

I am afraid, Father, that they will be swept away by waves of man-made reason and fall victim to the desires of their own fickle hearts. There's an audience and waiting applause for every action, no matter how far it takes them from You.

If they do find themselves lost in the shadowed forest of doubt and rebellion—a forest I know so well—Lord, call them home. Like You did for me.

Call them. They will know Your voice.

Please never stop chasing them.

I ask with the boldness of one who loves them with my little human love.

Never let them go.

Love,
ME

DEAR GOD,

If I hear one more fight today, I'm going to snap. How do You do it? Adults don't toss around insults like "poopyhead" and hide each other's toys; we spill blood. We invade boundaries. We claim human bodies as our own. How do You deal with our deadly conflict?

Do You cry? Do You bury Your head in Your hands and weep rainstorms? Do You shout the thunder? Does Your anger burn in streaks of hot lightning?

How You resist sending all of us to our permanent rooms, I'll never know.

Love,
ME

DEAR GOD,

I pray my children never believe
that where they happened to be born
makes them better than anyone else.

ME

DEAR GOD,

I research, fill out forms, add their names to lists, and scour the internet, trying to make the best choices, but I need You. Please bless my efforts. Nudge me in the right direction. Please blow on my dice because, to be honest, I have no idea what I'm doing.

Love,
ME

Dear God,

Please make my children the ones who sit next to the one who is alone. Stir in them a heart for the rejected. Heat in them a righteous desire to defend the ganged up on. Give them the bravery to say no when everyone is saying yes. Give them clear eyes and souls that long for justice and mercy.

Make me an example of all of the above.

Love,
Me

A Prayer for Mondays

Dear God,

Another week has begun,
and while to the untrained eye
I might seem brave
as I shuffle the calendar,
grow five arms, and juggle,
You know better.

My heart trembles.

Will this be another week
that chews me up
and spits me out
by five o'clock on Friday?

I don't pray for relief.
I don't pray for escape.

I don't pray for meals to
magically arrive—hot, nutritious,
and eaten without complaint by all—

I pray for the discipline
and desire
to stay in Your healing,
calming,
stilling
presence.

Help me stay here
in the garden.

When I'm in traffic,
battling for lane changes,
ten minutes behind schedule,

help me stay here
in the garden.

When I'm on the phone with a teacher,
worried about a child's future
and afraid,

help me stay here
in the garden.

When I'm standing over a hot stove,
pot bubbling,
dog barking,
children begging for snacks to sabotage their appetites,

help me stay here
in the garden.

When I'm tempted to leave
for the "greener" pastures of
control, anger, fear, resentment, and
overwhelm.

Take my hand
and lead me back
to the garden
with You.

Love,
ME

DEAR GOD,

If there are any sharp edges remaining on me, broken, pointed parts that may harm these children, please bring Your light and Your supernatural sander and smooth them into soft curves. Heal me so I can parent from a place of healing. Do not let me hurt them.

Do not let me hurt them.

Love,
ME

Dear God,

Long after the children go to sleep,
I position my feet on today's memory lane,
wishing I would have spoken softer,
played longer,

planted more flowers in their hearts
and fewer weeds of impatience,
rushing,
and curt answers to
innocent questions.

Please rain grace on today.
Let raindrops from heaven
form rivulets of living waters
that drip down their tender green leaves,
roll down their fragile shoots,
and pool around their roots,
nourishing them with everything
I ran out of and never had.

Let Your grace rain down on us
today and
forevermore.

Love,
Me

DEAR GOD,

I pray that it rains today so I can justify a nap. I'm beyond tired and need a month's worth of vacation days. But that won't happen, so please give me what I need to be all here.

There aren't enough positive affirmations, nights off, cups of strong drink, or books and movies to escape into to patch the holes inside my spirit.

I need Yours.

Please meet me where I am. Help me still this storm raging inside me so I can parent strong today.

I await the feeling of Your hands over mine.

Love,
ME

Dear God,

If there are stores of heavenly patience,
buckets filled to the brim with what I imagine
to be a butterscotch-hued, gently bubbling,
warm, and fragrant extract—
the essential oil of parenthood—
please pour it out on me.

Love,
Me

DEAR GOD,

Something about tonight made
moving the clothes from the
washer to dryer
feel like a herculean feat.

Please see me to the end of this evening.

It's not over yet.

Love,
ME

Dear God,

Sometimes this family of believers
feels very dysfunctional,
a body at war with itself
over power,
over influence.
Help us to love.
That's what You said,
"They will know you by your love"—
so our children can see that
Your love has changed us.
Help us.

Love,
Me

DEAR GOD,

Help me love these children's hearts
more than I idolize their potential,
more than I crave their performance.
You made them for more than good grades,
sports, and piano lessons.
Calm me.
Still me.
They are somebody today.
Don't let me get so caught up,
being afraid to mess up,
that I miss this time,
let it fly by
in a haze of errands,
appointments, and lessons.

ME

DEAR GOD,

How much You have trusted me
with the work of Your hands,

these tender, young hearts,
hungry minds,
and new souls.

You breathed life into this child
with purpose.

Help me to honor Your dreams
over mine

and to treat with care
and respect
this holy responsibility.

Help me.

Love,
ME

THANKS

Dear parent,

I often tell my children it's only after we leave this life that we will know all the things God has done for us.

The accidents averted. The blessings we chalked up to chance.

Thanking Him is important because it helps us remain in gratitude and remember that He is good. As I thank Him for everything about my children—from their curious eyes to their silly jokes, I'm reminded of how truly rich I am in the only way that matters.

Love, Bunmi

DEAR GOD,

One of my favorite things is when I'm bone-weary and You share some of Your love with me, just enough to get me to bedtime with a smile on my lips.

I know that's not me.

Because this love bears Your mark of deep peace and grace unrivaled. Thank You. Help me tonight again.

Love,
ME

DEAR GOD,

You are not the universe.
You created the universe.
You are not a passive, distant god.

You are a God who listens
and cares.

I prayed to You about my children,
brought my worries before You,

and You have answered me,
helped me,
comforted me,
stilled me.

Thank You for being the God of the big,
ever-expanding matter of a dark,
unknown universe.

And thank You for being the God of the small
matters of a parent
ever-fretting
over the unknown
in the dark.

Love,
ME

DEAR GOD,

Thank You for making me a parent. Thank You for giving me just a glimpse of how fierce and far-reaching Your love is. I know now that love means never giving up. Never giving in. I know what it is to love someone more than myself. I'm sorry for all the ways I've grieved You over the years because I know what that is too.

One day, God, in heaven let's talk about our kids over coffee. You and me.

Is it a date?

Love,
ME

DEAR GOD,

Thank You for:

teachers who care,
when we find a meal they actually like (for two weeks at
    least),
toddlers in splash pads,
four-year-olds in overalls,
the smile of sleeping infants,
taco night,
freshly bathed children,
the relief of Friday night,
the freedom of Saturday morning,
neighbors who don't mind a bit of noise.

Love,
ME

DEAR GOD,

In the scheme of things, the age difference between me and my children isn't that great. To You, it must be almost nothing.

Which explains why I feel like I'm winging it. I'm just barely ahead of them in understanding and stay up many nights cramming, preparing for tomorrow's tests.

God, we really are Your babies raising babies. Help us. We're winging it, making mistakes, and doing our best, which some days doesn't feel quite good enough.

I know it's Your grace alone covering us all and filling in the many gaps I leave undone in this patchwork of parenthood.

I know it's Your love that flows in my veins and makes another day of this possible.

Thank You. And never leave. Never. We both need You.

Love,
ME

DEAR GOD,

It must be human nature
to bite the hand that feeds us.

It's always the closest one.

No wonder children save
their worst behavior for their parents.

And we rage against the One who
created us.

The hand that is nearest
will always get bitten.

And yet it's the hand
that loves us the most.

Forgive us.

Love,
ME

DEAR GOD,

When I'm shuffling bills
and putting out work fires,
the last thing I want to do is
comfort a child whose
apple slices don't taste appley enough.

I'm doing important work,
the big work,
trying to keep us in this house
and the lights responding to
the flick of a switch.

And as I screamed internally,
I was reminded that
You keep the cosmos together,
prevent wars from breaking out,
Feed each and every bird,

and listen to me whine.

The remembrance of Your care
for my little things
gave me just enough grace

to spread peanut butter on a few crackers
in lieu of appley enough apples.

Thank You.

Love,
Me

DEAR GOD,

Thank You for waking us up,
sun gently streaming through the window,
bowls full of Cheerios and
bleary-eyed children,
white-blue morning sky.
I don't know what today holds,
but I know
You're in it.
Thank You.

Love,
ME

DEAR GOD,

Thank You for:

baby eyelashes,
dimpled smiles,
the steady breathing of deeply sleeping children,
the way their hand fits in mine,
the sound of siblings laughing about nonsense,
infant coos,
toddlers in onesie pajamas,
when they say a word wrong but we wouldn't change it for
    anything,
the way "mama" and "dada" sound coming out of their
    mouths,
the feeling of their little body in a bear hug,
baby smell,
the wildness of two-year-olds,
rainy days reading picture books,
the first giggle,
family movie night,
when they actually like dinner,
their faces as they sleep,
their first rain, snow, or beach,
the way they chase bubbles,

popsicles in paper towels on a summer day,
three-year-olds in rain boots,
teens who still need cuddles,

For all of that and more, thank You.

Love,
ME

DEAR GOD,

Thank You for microwaveable meals, pizza delivery, cereal, fruit cups, washers and dryers, friends who take the kids for a little while, strangers who become friends at the park, the day I slept until 9:00 a.m. last month, and all the little things that make life easier.

Thank You for the days that flow and the final "good night" of the day when I get to sink into my bed and just drift.

Thank You for the grace-soaked moments that keep us going. I can feel You in them.

Stay close to us and help us stay close to You. We won't get through this except by putting our hand in Yours.

ME

DEAR GOD,

Thank You for being the rising Spirit within me when I don't have the energy for another minute, another "look what I can do," another snack, or another game. Thank You for helping me rise to the needs until the sun and I set together. I know You are the power by which this home runs. I know because I am too tired to have made it this far on my own strength. You've picked me up more times than I know. You've gotten us through more long weekends—weekends that felt they would never end—more times than I know.

You've been the joy and have lit the laughter like the first spark of a bonfire more times than I know.

Thank You for being here.

Love,
ME

DEAR GOD,

As I walk through the valley of the shadow of
an uncertain future,
new and frightening news each day,
with lunches to pack
and floors to mop
and something in the oven,
hold still my heart.

My strength is knowing You are
here
and that as wave after wave comes
You stay by my side,
sometimes blocking the surging wall of water,
other times holding my head just above the surf.
But even on days I, submerged, am tossed by the
     undercurrent,
breath held, hair and clothes flowing around me,
suspended in ocean depths,
I hear You whispering in my ear
blessed assurances,
songs of hope,
promises of love,
and I rest.

Love,
ME

DEAR GOD,

There are days when I don't accomplish anything
the world would see as worthwhile.

I only wiped noses and counters,
moved wet laundry into the dryer,

put together unimpressive meals of cut-up fruit, meat slices,
crackers and cheese,

desperate charcuterie served in front of giant screens.

I didn't make a single dollar.

But I met the needs,
tried my best to listen to monologues about
games I don't play
and hugged.

No one will say "job well done"
or hand me a paycheck.
But I know You saw me.
I know You are pleased with me
for showing up, loving, trying.

And that's enough,
because doing things as for You,[*]
even if they're not good enough for Instagram,
makes them holy.

When You smile down on me
in my sweats and messy hair,

it's more than enough.

Thank You.

Love,
ME

---

* See Colossians 3:23.

Dear God,

Thank You for the answered prayer,
the one that descended on me so
softly
and perfectly
I forgot I'd ever lived without it.
Prayers answered so seamlessly
they feel deserved.

Forgive me for forgetting
to come back
and say thank You.

I say it now.
Thank You
so much.
Thank You.

Love,
Me

DEAR GOD,

I am pressed by impossible and always shifting to-dos: swimming lessons, teacher meetings, failed math quizzes, children who need face time, not FaceTime, and the laundry is growing and sentient. It yells at me.

Lord, You walked the earth when women beat clothes against the rocks and candles lit family rooms after dark. They managed.

Now with every convenience, I feel unarmed against life.

Take me to the Stone Age. Bring me to a simpler time in Your presence.

As I empty myself of my best perfume, let me sit at Your feet, bask in Your majesty, while the notifications go off untended.

It's You who holds my life together.

It's Your grace that slides every gear and bolt into place.

Like the parents of past, I continue to love, do laundry, and turn food over the fire, doing the things I must for those I love.

But it's You who keeps me afloat.

Thank You.

Love,
ME

Dear God,

Thank You for the moments
we see the baby in the growing boy,
the toddler in the teenage girl
for just a split second
as they turn their head this way
or smile just like that.
Surprise double feature—
it's breathtaking.

Love,
Me

DEAR GOD,

It really is incredible to watch them learn, grow,
struggle with something one day
and master it the next.
I hope I give You the same delight.

Love,
ME

Dear God,

Thank You for the uneventful days
when they leave for school and come back,
routine doctor's appointments,
boring Saturday mornings.
Because I know from the news
that these are unwrapped blessings,
tremendous gifts disguised as normalcy.
So thank You
very much
for regular days.

Love,
Me

DEAR GOD,

I'll never get tired of the
"just in time answered prayer" thing.
Thank You.

Love,
ME

DEAR GOD,

I can see changes.
I've been praying, and I see changes
emerging in this child,
flowers sprouting that I did not plant,
clouds parting that I did not blow away.
You did this.
Prayer is real.
You heard my cry.
Thank You
for Your love and help.
Thank You.

Love,
ME

DEAR GOD,

Parenting has taught me all the ways to say,
"I love you."

"I did the dishes."
"Dinner is ready."
"Your clothes are washed."
"I put away the towels."

Thank You for all the practical and faithful ways
You've told me You love me.

The ones I overlook and have come to expect.

Thank You for the sunrise,
another day, another chance.
Thank You for fresh, cool water
coming out of my tap.

Thank You for the millions of
things I've come to think I deserve
but are blessings
not all live with.

Help me be a blessing
to those in want.

Thank You.

Love,
ME

LAUGHTER

DEAR PARENT,

The hardest and funniest gig around. Sometimes all we can do is laugh, and that's okay.

LOVE, BUNMI

DEAR GOD,

Thank You for creating chickens,
without which
we would have no nuggets.

Love,
ME

Dear God,

It feels a little much that they need to eat three times a day. Including snacks, they eat every twenty-five minutes. How do I return them to factory settings? Please advise.

Me

Dear God,

Please bless the pizza delivery people
who pretend not to notice
this is the second time this week
and the frantic look in my eyes
and the way I must smell
and the stains on my hoodie.

They are heroes.
Please bless them.

Love,
Me

Dear God,

Did You intend for children to wake up so early, or are mine broken? Are there any updates I can download from Your cloud to get, say, one to three extra hours of REM for each of them? Is there a warranty I can inquire about or a manager I can speak to about this issue?

No one but roosters should be making noise before the sun comes up, yet here we are.

Is this a punishment? If so, I'm sorry.

Please send help.

Love,
Me

Dear God,

You created more than a
thousand types of vegetables,
leafy, sprouting, of all colors of the rainbow.
And yet every night I serve
baby carrots or cucumber slices.

This is my best.

Love,
Me

Dear God,

Why are middle children the way they are? These particular ones wake up every day and choose violence. The mouths on these kids. The energy level. The chaos.

Why? Please advise. We are tired. And a little bit afraid.

Love,
Me

DEAR GOD,

On the—

   tater tots
   microwaved quesadilla with string cheese
   chicken nuggets
   pizza rolls
   plates of cheese and apples
   hot dogs

—nights. Remind me that it's enough.

I'd make a casserole if I had one in me.

Love,
ME

DEAR GOD,

One of the main things I'm looking forward to in heaven is the absence of dirty dishes.

ME

DEAR GOD,

I'm so very grateful for the food You have provided, but I won't have to make dinner in heaven, right?

Love,
ME

Dear God,

If parenting has taught me anything,
it's that I'm not You
and I need You,
because if I have to make one more snack today,
it will be Your strength, not mine, that spreads the peanut
    butter
on the saltines.
Thanks for being there in the little things too.

Love,
Me

DEAR GOD,

I either need more coffee
or less day.

Love,
ME

DEAR GOD,

I know revenge is Yours alone,[*]
but did You have to give
this child the same flavor of
attitude as me?
This mirror is humbling.
Maybe that was the point.

Strength please.

Love,
ME

---

* See Romans 12:19.

DEAR GOD,

Are there angels available who mop floors?
Asking for a friend.

Love,
ME

DEAR GOD,

Just so You know.
When I'm shaking with frustration and tell my child,
"If you would have just listened the first time,"
I can hear You laughing.

Love,
ME

DEAR GOD,

I'm so tired of cooking. Takeout for one night costs almost half a grocery trip. Please forgive me for being such a bad steward. In my Father's house are many mansions.*

That said, can You handle tonight's bill?

Love,
ME

---

* See John 14:2.

DEAR GOD,

I wasn't there when You gave her
that attitude,
that spice,
that fight.
I know it was for a good reason.
There are battles she'll need these weapons
to win.
But in the meantime—
HELP!

ME

DEAR GOD,

It's almost seven, and I haven't made dinner yet. I haven't even thought of dinner. It'd be real nice to be able to say something like, "Let there be chicken strips," and have a meal appear. Must be nice to have all those powers . . . but then again, I wouldn't want Your job. Too many kids. I hope You're okay.

Love,
ME

DEAR GOD,

Do You keep a scrapbook?
A bursting-at-the-seams collection of Your favorite photos
    of us
with hand-scrawled dates and locations?
Or is the Bible Your only family album?
Genuinely curious.

Love,
ME

DEAR GOD,

I agree with the children about eggplant.
Just for the record.
No offense intended.

Love,
ME

DEAR GOD,

I know it's a blessing to have clothes,
but sometimes it feels like the laundry is multiplying
like the loaves and fish.*

Love,
ME

---

* See Mark 6:30–44.

*D*EAR *G*OD,

What's it like having seven billion children, give or take?
It's a good thing You invented electricity;
the bill would be enormous.
If anyone deserves a day off, it's You.
Thanks for not giving up on us.

Love,
*M*E

DEAR GOD,

Sometimes I get angry about
empty containers in the pantry,
jam on the counter,
dirty socks on the floor.
And then I'm reminded that
we've left quite the mess on the planet You made.
Sorry.
I know there are no paper towels big enough for this.

Love,
ME

DEAR GOD,

The most amazing thing
about heaven to me
is that it never needs washing—
not a dirty dish, crumb, or dust ball in sight.
If that were not the case,
it wouldn't be heaven
(please let that be the case).

Love,
ME

DEAR GOD,

After taking my family on a road trip
for just one weekend,
I can't even imagine what
forty days and forty nights on that boat was like for Noah.

ME

DEAR GOD,

Last weekend I took my kids on a walk.
It was less than twenty minutes there and back,
but I'm not doing it again.
If You see Moses today,
give him a hug from me.

Love,
ME

Dear God,

I don't know if You're taking requests
but a vegetable that tastes like chicken nuggets
would help me out tremendously.

Thank You.

Love,
Me

DEAR GOD,

I read this today:
"In Eden, Adam and Eve were naked.
It wasn't until they sinned that they were clothed.
Therefore, laundry was part of the fall."
I believe it.

Love,
ME

DEAR GOD,

Do You hide food the way we do?
But instead of chocolate chips behind canned beans
and secret potato chips in the nightstand,
do You have a place You go that we don't know about?
Another galaxy perhaps for a weary Father?
Secret bouquets of unknown Milky Ways and
black holes swirling with purples, blues, and celestial dust?
Unrevealed sunsets or music notes and instruments
unheard of?

I hope so. Because secret chocolate is the
best chocolate.

Love,
ME

TEENS

It seems only yesterday we held their chubby toddler hands in ours. Now the endless chatter of a small child who wanted to tell us everything has been replaced with a rapidly growing teen caught between childhood and adulthood—head bowed over their illuminated phone. They have secrets, their own friends, and their own lives. There's no need to arrange playdates ("pick up and drop off, please!").

It's normal . . . but scary.

Will they remember what we taught them?

Will they make good choices?

Who will protect them from what lurks in the shadows?

We don't have the control we once had. But while there is so often a closed bedroom door between you and your child these days, there is always an open invitation to the throne room.

Our prayers are to a God who is not limited by closed doors or fazed by raging hormones. We can cover our teens in a blanket of heavenly beseeching, no matter where they are and what they're going through.

Remember, He loved them first. He has plans for them. We are never expected to raise them without the help of the One who knit their soul together. In truth, we are temporary custodians of these children who, like us, belong to the divine hand that formed them. Slightly older babies raising babies.

So we do our best. We keep the pantry stocked with snacks and the lectures poignant but short to avoid glazed-over eyes and impatient huffs. But the most powerful tool in our parenting arsenal is heaven-sent.

Prayer. We need help. And we have help.

Love, Bunmi

Dear God,

They so want to fit in,
but You made them to stand out
in a time when conformity is rewarded.
The ability to follow the steady
rhythm of the latest twenty-six-second dance
is praised.
Help them to know when to break away
and move to the beat You placed within them.
Help them hear Your song,
and give them the strength to be
set apart.

Love,
Me

DEAR GOD,

Long gone are the days
when their chubby hands
are safe in mine at every
intersection.

They cross the street alone now,
rub shoulder to shoulder with
stranger danger.

They see excitement.
I see risk.

Help me to let go
a little bit
so their wings can stretch,
grow,
test the air currents.

It's scary,
but I'll get through it
with my chubby little hand
in Yours.

Love,
ME

DEAR GOD,

I remember when they used to
tell me so much,
my brain felt like melted wax
by 4:00 p.m.—
nonstop chatter
about pine cones,
cookies, raindrops,
the little girl next door,
rainbows, butterflies,
construction sites.

These days it's so quiet.
As their thoughts have grown deeper,
their words have become fewer.

I feel like a fisherman
daily casting long lines,
hoping for a bite.

I know it's normal,
and a sparkling gem—
every sentence spoken
a deep-sea treasure,
even when it's
"Can I have five dollars?"

It only reminds me
that maybe
You'd like to hear from me more.

Love,
Me

DEAR GOD,

It's hard but wonderful,
watching them grow
into beautiful flowers,

little sprouts becoming
towering bamboo palms,

baby buds into
the wide leaves of
fiddle leaf figs.

Now, just as before,
I need You to garden
alongside me.

Because what do I know
about big plants?

ME

Dear God,

I believe You must
have a legion of angels
just for teenagers

to bridge the gap
when terrible decisions
are made.

Whisper reminders to
shower.

The powerful beating of wings
to temper
hormonal thunderstorms.

Release more, please,
over them
from dawn to dusk
and through the night.
Let Your warriors of light
bring Your presence,
power, grace, and love.

Let them never be without
help from heaven.

Love,
ME

Dear God,

It's hard to believe that
in Jesus' days on earth
teens were married,
but then again it makes sense.

They'd be too busy
changing diapers and
making a living
to get into any serious trouble.

Maybe they had the right idea
all along.

But no grandkids yet, please.

Love,
Me

DEAR GOD,

One day I'd like to know
where the idea for black holes
came from and if any of my
cutlery is in there.

ME

DEAR GOD,

Life is full of so many mysteries.

But right now I'd just like to know
why they leave so many
cups in their bedrooms.

Love,
ME

DEAR GOD,

I know that school bullies
are often bullied themselves,
but that doesn't stop me
from wanting to fight a child.

Please give me wisdom
and grace,
or bail money—

any combination would suffice

ME

DEAR GOD,

There's that one friend—
the one I can see
is hell-bent
on leading them down
the darkest of alleys.

My prayer is for my child
and for this child.

Please keep mine safe.
Give them discernment,
wisdom,
courage to say no
when I'm not there.

And for this
lost lamb
headed toward
all manner of cliffs.

You, Lord, are my Shepherd.
Please be theirs too.

Love,
ME

Dear God,

Help me to know when to
lay down the law
and when to extend the same grace
You've shown me,

when to speak truth loudly
and when to whisper
to You in my prayer closet,

when to stage a rescue operation
and when to put it in
Your hands.

Help me to know.

Love,
Me

Dear God,

Thank You for being my
eyes and ears,
my early warning system
alerting me to things
I need to address,
nip in the bud,
call out,
and correct.

I could not parent
without You.

Love,
Me

Dear God,

When the week is too long,
when the demands won't stop,
when I'm running out of love,
when my patience is wearing thin,
when I feel I'm giving from my very marrow . . .

lead me to the Rock that is higher than I.*

Love,
Me

---

* Psalm 61:2.

Dear God,

I know You are here because
somehow the most important
work gets done.

Somehow we get
through another week
intact.

Somehow the pieces
fall into place.

I know You are in that
somehow.

Thank You.

Love,
Me

REMINDERS FOR HARD TIMES

Dear parent,

I wrote this section for the hard days and moments of parenting, of which there are many. As I said before, it's my relationship with the living God through Jesus that is my rock in this life. Communication through prayer is key, but as it is in any relationship, we have to listen as much as, if not more than, we talk. And He speaks.

While I've had amazing dreams, even visions, the number-one way God speaks to me is through the Bible. Some think of it as an old, albeit important, but out-of-date book, but when I tell you it is alive and He speaks through it to those who are willing to open its pages . . . well, that you will have to find out for yourself.

On my most difficult days, the ones where my heart and mind are heavy with doubt, fear, and frustration, it's God's gentle reminders, promises, and guidance through this book that is alive as you and me that keep me not just afloat but soaring on wings like an eagle.

Here are a few of the verses that feed me living water daily.

Love, Bunmi

Psalm 121

Psalm 121, written by King David, is one of the first passages I committed to memory, not on purpose, but because I recited it over and over, with eyes stretched toward the horizon. I have a favorite mountainous area in Quebec—a town called Sutton. It's beautiful. In the winter, the mountains are covered with blankets of white snow. In the summer, they're alive with bright green grass and wildflowers and cows and horses roaming. And in the fall, when life begins to grow quiet due to the chilly winds cutting through our sweaters, the brilliant colors of autumn—crimson, pumpkin, and caramel leaves—delight the eyes and soul.

Whatever season of life you are in, I hope this psalm reminds you that you are never alone. God is here, and He will preserve your soul.

Psalm 121

I lift up my eyes to the hills.
From where does my help come?
My help comes from the LORD,
who made heaven and earth.

He will not let your foot be moved;
    he who keeps you will not slumber.
Behold, he who keeps Israel
    will neither slumber nor sleep.

The LORD is your keeper;
    the LORD is your shade on your right hand.
The sun shall not strike you by day,
    nor the moon by night.

The LORD will keep you from all evil;
    he will keep your life.
The LORD will keep
    your going out and your coming in
    from this time forth and forevermore.

Jeremiah 1:4-5

Jeremiah was a prophet to the nation of Israel. He is called the "weeping prophet" because his burden was heavy; the news he came to bring was not good. He had a tender heart and was grieved for his people in the same way God was.

Maybe you're grieving now. Maybe you've received bad news. Maybe you're in the middle of a time so thick with sorrow and woe that it's hard to believe the sun could ever rise again.

These verses describe God's calling of Jeremiah to be who he was—the time when Jeremiah was given a very difficult job. He didn't think he was up to the task, but God let him know that he was known to Him and therefore could do what He was calling him to.

I don't know what you're going through, but I do know that your life is no accident. The lives of your children are not accidents. Just as God knew you before you were born, He knew them as well.

In that knowledge, we can find a measure of rest. Not necessarily peace, but rest, because God has always known us and knows what we would carry one day.

May your burden grow lighter by knowing He knows you and yours.

JEREMIAH 1:4–5

Then the word of the LORD came to me, saying:

"Before I formed you in the womb I knew you;
Before you were born I sanctified you."*

---

* NKJV.

Isaiah 43:1-3

Last year, I started watching a television series called *The Chosen*, which changed my life. I had known the Bible stories and watched many depictions of them, but this show brought them to life in a way I'd never experienced.

The Chosen's first episode refers to the first few verses of Isaiah 43, which speak of a God who is deeply protective of His own. Every time I read them, my heart clenches with deep emotion, and I am moved by His fierce and protective love for us.

What could come between you and your child? Roaring waves? A wall of fire? A wild animal? Chances are, we'd do our best to run through them.

How much more so, then, would the God of the universe guard our souls?

Things happen in life. So many things happen to us and our children. But the Keeper of our souls promises to walk with us through them.

In the episode of *The Chosen*, the character, Mary, is taught this verse by her father while she is young, and she recites it when she's deeply troubled. Many years later, when life gets unbearable, she keeps the words nearby—written on a scrap of parchment— and clings to them when she needs them the most.

Teach these verses to your little ones so they know, no matter what, that they are never alone.

Isaiah 43:1–3

"Fear not, for I have redeemed you;
    I have called you by name, you are mine.
When you pass through the waters, I will be with you;
    and through the rivers, they shall not overwhelm you;
when you walk through fire you shall not be burned,
    and the flame shall not consume you.
For I am the LORD your God,
    the Holy One of Israel, your Savior."

PSALM 23

In a book of poetry, I wrote, "Parenting has a way of filling us up and draining us at the same time."

It's like that.

The joy is intense and life-giving, but by the end of the day, I don't know about you, but I'm depleted. I'm done. I feel as if I gave from the very marrow of my bones, and then a bit more.

Once the children are in bed, strange feelings can descend on us, along with the fatigue—anger, resentment, depression. Giving so much is hard, and it has a way of making this life of taking care of a family unsustainable.

I used to think the answer was a nightcap or television. And while I sometimes do zone out for hours, mindlessly scrolling, trying to revive what I lost during the day, it's only ever been the Sustainer who has restored my soul.

Psalm 23 paints a gorgeous picture of a lush valley, sparkling fresh rivers of life-giving waters, and a Shepherd who cares for His weary sheep.

I read this psalm, and let every word come alive in my mind when I need life. New life. A life infusion that can't be found anywhere else (I've looked). I read it over and over again. I pray it. I ask God to pour life into my tired soul, and whether the answer comes in a cup of tea and hours of sleep or my awareness of His presence entering my bedroom and touching my heart, He answers.

My prayer is for your soul's rest. Well done today.

Psalm 23

The LORD *is* my shepherd; I shall not want.
   He makes me lie down in green pastures.
He leads me beside still waters.
   He restores my soul.
He leads me in paths of righteousness
   for his name's sake.
Even though I walk through the valley of the shadow of
   death,
   I will fear no evil,
for you are with me;
   your rod and your staff,
   they comfort me.
You prepare a table before me
   in the presence of my enemies;
you anoint my head with oil;
   my cup overflows.
Surely goodness and mercy shall follow me
   all the days of my life,
and I shall dwell in the house of the LORD
   forever.

Matthew 7:13-14

The first time I had to say no to my child when it seemed like everyone else was saying yes was very hard. Going with the flow is easy; friends stay, family agrees, and kids smile. But in this life, we're promised a difficult, opposition-filled path when we follow God's leading for ourselves, our families, and our children.

So when you're feeling alone because you had to step off the wide path, it doesn't mean anything is wrong. When your child angrily slams the door because they can't go to the party, it doesn't mean you're a bad parent. Take heart. Pray. Ask God for comfort for you and the child who doesn't understand today but might tomorrow, next year, or when they have children of their own.

Matthew 7:13–14

Enter by the narrow gate; for wide is the gate and broad is the way that leads to destruction, and there are many who go in by it. Because narrow is the gate and difficult is the way which leads to life, and there are few who find it.*

---

* NKJV.

ROMANS 8:37-39

Despite the beautiful scenery, this life is not a walk in the park. On days when dinner is burning on the stove, children are in crisis, marriages are on the brink, and it feels as though rock after giant rock is rolling down your mountains, taking aim at your peace, I remember that the Spirit in me cannot be overpowered by circumstances.

Me on my own, yes, I can crumble. I cry and fall apart in the bathroom. But the Spirit of God in me is a warrior, and so I am a warrior.

And more than that, I am seen, known, and loved by God.

All of this means two things: today cannot conquer me, and God is with me.

Let this knowledge sink into you. Ask Him for help and know that help is coming. And in the meantime, whether you feel it or not, you are His, and you are loved.

ROMANS 8:37–39

Yet in all these things we are more than conquerors through Him who loved us. For I am persuaded that neither death nor life, nor angels nor principalities nor powers, nor things present nor things to come, nor height nor depth, nor any other created thing, shall be able to separate us from the love of God which is in Christ Jesus our Lord.*

EPHESIANS 6:14-18

Every morning, I pray for the full armor of God for myself and my family. When we walk out into the world, we walk into a spiritual battle. Yes, we have fun, we delight and wonder and laugh, but we also fight things both seen and unseen.

A soldier without armor is unprotected. In the same way that we wouldn't let our kids walk into a snowstorm without a warm coat and good boots, equipping them with the spiritual tools they need today is a crucial part of being a parent of faith. It won't happen overnight, but as you pray and seek God for yourself, He'll reveal just how to lead your children on their path.

You've got this.

EPHESIANS 6:14–18

Stand therefore, having girded your waist with truth, having put on the breastplate of righteousness, and having shod your feet with the preparation of the gospel of peace; above all, taking the shield of faith with which you will be able to quench all the fiery darts of the wicked one. And take the helmet of salvation, and the sword of the Spirit, which is the word of God; praying always with all prayer and supplication in the Spirit, being watchful to this end with all perseverance and supplication for all the saints.*

* NKJV.

2 Timothy 1:7

Whether it's a bump in the night or beginning their high school adventures, all children will contend with fear. Cuddles and warm assurances by a loving parent are wonderful, but the truths in the Bible, the promises of God, have made such a difference in helping my children put on their divine armor against battles of the mind.

I taught my youngest this verse, and he uses it like a sword, without my help, when something frightens him.

It's good for adults too.

2 Timothy 1:7

For God gave us a spirit not of fear but of power and love and self-control.

ACKNOWLEDGMENTS

Thank you, God, for never letting go.

Thank you, J, for helping bring out the prayer warrior in me.

Thank you, kids, for helping me become the woman I am and for being so cute.

Thank you, Holly, for always being my advocate.

Thank you, Carolyn, for believing in me.

Thank you, Dirk, for your perfectly timed blessings.

Thank you, Katie, for your fiercely smart and kind leadership.

Thank you, Zondervan, for taking such good care of me.

Thank you to my mom and dad for doing their best during such hard times. I love you both.

Dear God

Honest Prayers to a God Who Listens

Bunmi Laditan

Dear God is a poignant collection of funny, often heartbreaking, and deeply insightful letters to God that bravely share the emotions we all feel as we grapple with this broken world and search for divine love.

With gutsy and poetic honesty, Bunmi shares prayers and poems that chart her faith journey toward reconnecting with the God she loved, lost, and realized had never left her side even while she wandered. These candid field notes will stir your heart and make you laugh out loud with Bunmi's self-aware humor and profound insight into the spiritual journey we're all trying to navigate.

Join Bunmi as she journeys through emotions we all experience—doubt, anger, joy, desperation, love, loneliness, and gratefulness. Wittingly fresh and stunningly relatable, she exquisitely names our fears, voices our painful questions, and bravely says what we're all thinking anyway in our prayerful wrestling with God.

This poignant collection of prayers is a strengthening reminder that the same Love that rises and sets the sun cares for you with particular affection.

Available in stores and online!